To: Verra ~

Peace Be With You

From: Ena ~
with Love.

Poppy: Liz Edwards

Jude 1:2
May mercy, peace, and love be yours in full measure.
(Good News Bible)

1 Corinthians 1:3

My prayer is that God our Father and the Lord
Jesus Christ will be kind to you and will bless
you with peace!

(Contemporary English Version)

•

Psalm 122:7

Peace be within your walls,
Prosperity within your palaces.

(New King James Version)

Job 37:14
Stand still and consider the wondrous
works of God.
(New King James Version)

●

The wonder and beauty of creation
never fails to lift one's spirit,
especially if in the lifting
we thank the Creator!
Anon

Beside the Lake: Sheila Adams

Find peace in creation...

I see skies of blue, and clouds of white.
The bright blessed day, the dark sacred night
And I think to myself... what a wonderful world...

Bob Thiele and George David Weiss
Recorded by Louis Armstrong (1968)

Sunburst over Lake Garda: Joseph Proctor

Matthew 11:28
Come to me, all you who are weary and burdened,
and I will give you rest.

(New International Version)

●

Let God's promises shine on your problems...
Corrie ten Boom
Dutch writer and concentration camp survivor, 1892-1983

●

A problem is a chance for you to do your best.
Duke Ellington
American jazz composer and performer, 1899-1974

●

When you make a stupid mistake, ask yourself,
"Will this really matter twenty years from now?"

If you can find a path with no obstacles, it probably doesn't lead anywhere.

Anon

•

When one door closes, another opens. But we often look so regretfully upon the closed door that we don't see the one that has opened for us.

Helen Keller
American deaf-blind writer and advocate for the disabled, 1880-1968

There is no problem too knotty for God to unravel.

I know that God will not give me anything I can't handle.
I just wish that He didn't trust me so much.
Mother Teresa
Catholic nun and advocate for the poor, 1910-1997

Rope: Liz Edwards

Find peace
despite your worries...

Don't hurry. Don't worry.
Do your best and let it rest.

•

Worry is like a rocking chair, it gives you
something to do, but it gets you nowhere.
Glenn Turner
New Zealand cricketer, 1947-present

•

1 Peter 5:7
God cares for you, so turn all your
worries over to him.
(Contemporary English Version)

On the Lake: Tim Fuller

Our life is frittered away by detail…
simplify, simplify.
Henry David Thoreau
American author, 1817-1862

•

Worry does not empty tomorrow of its sorrows,
it empties today of its strength.
Corrie ten Boom
Dutch writer and concentration camp survivor, 1892-1983

Sailing Boat: Joseph Proctor

Do not worry!

Matthew 6:25-27

Therefore I tell you, do not worry about your life,
what you will eat or drink; or about your body, what you will wear.
Is not life more important than food,
and the body more important than clothes?
Look at the birds of the air;
they do not sow or reap or store away in barns,
and yet your heavenly Father feeds them.
Are you not much more valuable than they?
Who of you by worrying can add a single hour to his life?

(New International Version)

Blue Tit: Mary Hallett

Find peace
through prayer...

Any concern too small to be turned into a prayer
is too small to be made into a burden.

Corrie Ten Boom
Clippings From My Notebook

●

Lord of calm and storm,
I come to you for peace of mind.

Eddie Askew
Christian writer and former International Director
of TLM, 1927-2007

●

Philippians 4:6-7
Do not be anxious about anything, but in
everything, by prayer and petition, with
thanksgiving, present your requests to God.
And the peace of God, which transcends all
understanding, will guard your hearts and your
minds in Christ Jesus.

(New International Version)

Boats on Vils Alp Lake, Austrian Tyrol: Norma Darey

Prayer should be the key of the day
And the lock of the night.

Thomas Fuller
English writer, 1608-1661

•

The best prayers are often more groans than words!

John Bunyan
English writer, 1628-1688

The Jetty at Dusk: Tim Fuller

The Prayer of St Francis

Lord, make me an instrument
of your peace,
Where there is hatred, let me sow love;
where there is injury, pardon;
where there is doubt, faith;
where there is despair, hope;
where there is darkness, light;
where there is sadness, joy;
O Divine Master,
Grant that I may not so much seek to be consoled
as to console;
to be understood as to understand;
to be loved as to love.
For it is in giving that we receive;
it is in pardoning that we are pardoned;
and it is in dying that we are born to eternal life.

Snowy Gateway: Sheila Adams

The Serenity Prayer

God grant me the serenity
to accept the things I cannot change;
courage to change the things I can;
and wisdom to know the difference.
Living one day at a time;
enjoying one moment at a time;
accepting hardships as the pathway to peace;
taking, as He did, this sinful world
as it is, not as I would have it;
trusting that He will make all things right
if I surrender to His Will;
that I may be reasonably happy in this life
and supremely happy with Him
forever in the next.
Amen.

Reinhold Niebuhr
American theologian, 1892-1971

Poppies: Liz Edwards

Glorious silence...

Spend a few minutes every day without
conversation, music or the news.
Revel in the pleasure of it.
Listen to God.
Anon

•

Philippians 4:8-9
…Whatever is true, whatever is noble, whatever is right,
whatever is pure, whatever is lovely, whatever is admirable –
if anything is excellent or praiseworthy – think about such things.
Whatever you have learned or received or heard from me, or seen in me –
put it into practice. And the God of peace will be with you.

(New International Version)

Dewdrops: Steve Cocking

Find peace in God...

Teach me, my God and King
In all things thee to see,
And what I do in anything,
To do it as for thee.

George Herbert
Clergyman and poet, 1593–1633

●

Romans 15:13
I pray that God, the source of hope,
will fill you completely with joy and peace
because you trust in him.
Then you will overflow with confident hope
through the power of the Holy Spirit.

(New Living Translation)

Church Window: Mary Hallett

Deuteronomy 31:8

Do not be afraid or discouraged, for the LORD will personally go ahead of you. He will be with you; he will neither fail you nor abandon you.

(New Living Translation)

●

Hebrews 13:5

Never will I leave you; never will I forsake you.

(New International Version)

●

When life was tough, I would use my fingers to
spell out the words
I WILL NEVER LEAVE YOU
silently in my pocket, on the desk, wherever –
and slowly my peace of mind returned
along with the knowledge that
NOTHING
is impossible for God.

Liz Edwards

Frozen Leaves: Mary Hallett

Find peace in Jesus...

Turn your eyes upon Jesus,
Look full in His wonderful face,
And the things of earth will grow strangely dim,
In the light of His glory and grace.

Helen H. Lemmel
British-American hymn writer, 1863-1961

Buttercup: Liz Edwards

I'm special because God has loved me,
For He gave the best thing that He had to save me.
His own Son Jesus, crucified to take the blame,
For all the bad things I have done.

Graham Kendrick
British songwriter, 1950-present

Cross: Liz Edwards

Release the past and find peace...

When the Japanese mend broken objects,
they aggrandize the damage by filling the cracks with gold.
They believe that when something's suffered damage
and has a history it becomes more beautiful.
Barbara Bloom
American sculptor, 1951- present

•

The problems, worries and difficulties
that we encounter and overcome
make us the people that we are:
mature, experienced, beautiful.

•

The past is history.
The future is a mystery.
And this moment is a gift.
That is why this moment is called 'the present'.
Anon

And finally...

Every evening I turn my worries over to God.
He's going to be up all night anyway.

Mary C. Crowley
American businesswoman, 1915-1986

Sunset: Joseph Proctor

Perfect endings? I've learned the hard way,
that some stories don't have a clear beginning,
middle and end. Life is about taking one step at a
time, not knowing the outcome or even the journey!

●

Do not be afraid of tomorrow for
God is already there.

Anon

John 14:27

I am leaving you with a gift –
peace of mind and heart.
And the peace I give
is a gift the world cannot give.
So don't be troubled or afraid.

(New Living Translation)

Country Road: Joseph Proctor